# LEARNING TO LOVE ME
## While Putting the Pieces Back Together

**JOANNE McCRAE**

©Copyright 2020 Joanne McCrae

All rights reserved. This book is protected under the copyright laws of the United States of America.

**ISBN-13:** 978-1-7351126-5-7

No portion of this book may be reproduced, distributed, or transmitted in any form, including photocopying, recording, or other electronic or mechanical methods, without the written permission of the publisher, except in the case of brief quotations embodied in reviews and certain other non-commercial uses permitted by copyright law. Permission granted on request.

For information regarding special discounts for bulk purchases, please contact the publisher: LaBoo Publishing Enterprise, LLC

staff@laboopublishing.com
www.laboopublishing.com

Scripture quotations marked (NIV) are taken from the Holy Bible, New International Version®, NIV®. Copyright © 1973, 1978, 1984, 2011 by Biblica, Inc.™ Used by permission of Zondervan. All rights reserved worldwide. www.zondervan.com

Scripture taken from the New King James Version®. Copyright © 1982 by Thomas Nelson. Used by permission. All rights reserved.

*The Holy Bible, King James Version*. Cambridge Edition: 1769; *King James Bible Online*, 2019. www.kingjamesbibleonline.org.

The Living Bible copyright © 1971 by Tyndale House Foundation. Used by permission of Tyndale House Publishers Inc., Carol Stream, Illinois 60188. All rights reserved. The Living Bible, TLB, and The Living Bible logo are registered trademarks of Tyndale House Publishers.

Any references or similarities to actual real people, are intended to give the novel a sense of reality. Any similarity in names, or characters is entirely coincidental.

I give this book, *Learning to Love Me, While Putting the Pieces Back Together*, back to my Heavenly Father. I want to thank my family and friends for allowing me to be me. I want to thank my mentor Cheryl A.S. Hurley for being able to see the hidden author in me. Thank you, Cheryl!

# CONTENTS

Introduction . . . . . . . . . . . . . . . . . . . . . . . . . . . . . . . . . . . . . . . . vii

Chapter 1: Relationships Between Men & Women . . . . . . . . . . . . . . 1

Chapter 2: Crossing the Line . . . . . . . . . . . . . . . . . . . . . . . . . . . . . . 9

Chapter 3: The Danger of Crossing the Line in the Spirit Realm: *Transferring Spirits through the Hymen*. . . . . . . . . . . . . . . . . . 13

Chapter 4: The Miscarriage: *Aborting the Baby (God's Vision)*. . . . 17

Chapter 5: Will You Be Made Whole?. . . . . . . . . . . . . . . . . . . . . . . 21

Chapter 6: Who Am I?. . . . . . . . . . . . . . . . . . . . . . . . . . . . . . . . . . 27

Chapter 7: When You Think He's the Right One . . . . . . . . . . . . . . 31

Chapter 8: So Close but Not Yet. . . . . . . . . . . . . . . . . . . . . . . . . . . 35

Chapter 9: Marriage is a Covenant. . . . . . . . . . . . . . . . . . . . . . . . . 39

Chapter 10: Are You Really Ready?. . . . . . . . . . . . . . . . . . . . . . . . 41

Chapter 11: While You Are Waiting . . . . . . . . . . . . . . . . . . . . . . . 43

Chapter 12: Staying Focused............................45

Chapter 13: Going to the Next Level......................47

About the Author......................................51

# INTRODUCTION

It gives me pleasure to be able to reflect on my hurts and disappointments, knowing that each experience will be an encouragement to others. It was hard to write and share, but my Heavenly Father gave me the scripture Psalm 45:1 (NIV), "My heart is stirred by a noble theme as I recite my verses for the king; my tongue is the pen of a skillful writer." Once I came to myself, I no longer allowed a man to treat me the way he wanted to. It was good to be afflicted because it shaped me to be the strong woman I am today (Psalm 119:71).

The purpose of writing *Learning to Love Me, While Putting the Pieces Back Together* is to stress to fathers the significant role they play in their daughters' lives. I also want young ladies and older ladies to understand the importance of their self-worth.

My life started in broken pieces because of the absence of my father. I remember that diamond in the rough called Joanne. I was lost and broken and needed repair. As I walked through the process of becoming the diamond that I was destined to be, my name changed from Joanne to Gem. I am a gem because God paid the price for me to walk in purity. I could not remain silent, knowing that iron sharpens iron, as referenced in Proverbs 27:17. I have found that I can help deliver my sisters. I understand how Jeremiah felt in the scripture passage Jeremiah 20:9 when he said, "It was in my heart like a burning fire shut up in my bones."

## *Chapter 1*

# RELATIONSHIPS BETWEEN MEN & WOMEN

I am going to start by saying that my experience in life called me to become set apart. The first sign of this call appeared because I was tired of having unfaithful relationships with men. I praise God that my experiences did not cause me to have a relationship with another woman. The second sign of this call to be set apart was that I began to apply God's word to my life. The importance of waiting for marriage is in accordance with Romans 12: 1-2 (KJV), which says, "I beseech you therefore, brethren by the mercies of God, that ye present your bodies a living sacrifice, holy, acceptable unto God, which is your reasonable service. And do not be conformed to this world, but be transformed by the renewing of your mind, that you may prove what is that good and acceptable and perfect will of God." Another scripture that aligns with the importance of waiting for marriage is Hebrews 13:4 (NKJV), which says, "Marriage is honorable among all, and the bed undefiled; but fornicators and adulterers God will judge." "For this you know, that no fornicator, unclean person, nor covetous man, who is an idolater, has any inheritance in the kingdom of Christ and God. Let no one deceive you with empty words, for because of these things the wrath of God comes upon the sons of disobedience. Therefore, do not be partakers with them" Ephesians 5: 5-7 (NKJV).

I started dating at the age of 15. I became a mother at the age of 16. I finished high school and received my diploma. It took me some years to come to my senses to stop looking for love. Looking for love has caused me emotional pain because of the rejection I experienced as a child from my father. It affected me for many, many years. I praise God that I did not experience physical or emotional abuse in any of my relationships. I have a few questions for you. What is love? How do you know if you are in love with a person? Are you compromising because you are afraid of being alone? I can tell you briefly what love is not. Love is not selfish. By allowing a man to become the center of your attention, you unintentionally make things all about him. Love is God-centered. God said in Mark 3:35 (NKJV), "For whoever does the will of God is My brother and My sister and mother." That leads me to ask a question. Brothers, how are you treating your sisters? I raised my son Steve to treat women the same way he would want a man to treat me. Love is not using God's word to get a woman in bed.

Love is not controlling. Love is not manipulative or deceitful. Attempting to get someone to do what you want them to do is not love. Love is not lying your way into someone's life by painting a pretty picture. Love is not seeking a relationship with a person who is established in hope of financial gain. Love is not receiving money here and there and being used or mistreated. Love is not having a Christian man tell you that having sex one time won't hurt because you could always repent afterwards.

I was dating a man named Wade. Wade once suggested that he and I have sex and then repent together. I looked at him, totally confused, and said, "Are you crazy"? His response was, "You don't love me, Joanne." I remained silent. I was solid in my position and I did not bend. Love is not intimidated by your spiritual walk with God. It will not try to distract you from your purpose or your Heavenly Father.

That's enough of what love is not. As people, we play a big part in what others do to us. Please understand that people can only do what we allow them to do. Be very careful when people tell you up front that you are just a friend. They want to keep their options open for others who will give them what they want. It is imperative to seek your Higher power for a relationship, especially if you are considering taking their last name. You want someone who you find attractive, has wisdom, and is not afraid to be themselves with you.

Pay attention to what's being said to you without making excuses for negative behavior. Be open to hear what he or she is not saying without making excuses for them. Satan has studied you. He knows exactly what you desire. If you don't trust your own judgment in a friendship, invite your friend to a family/friend event and ask your loved ones for feedback.

People can come wearing masks. Not being able to discern people and their intentions could cause you to abort your mission from your Higher Power. We all have a purpose, to serve in God's kingdom. Matthew 6:33 (KJV) says, "But seek first the kingdom of God and his righteousness, and all these things shall be added unto you." It's easy for women to become distracted for several reasons. One reason is vulnerability. For example, a single mother who wants a father figure for her child/children can be very vulnerable. She may be financially struggling. While looking for that father figure, she may decide to move in with a person she barely knows. Within two to three months of dating, she realizes that she is putting her child's life in danger. She goes to work and leaves her child/children home with him. As soon as she leaves the house to go to work, he gets into bed with the child. That child is now damaged and could be destroyed for the rest of his/her life because the mother failed to wait for God to send her a mate.

This is a worst-case scenario, but it is a very realistic example of what happens when we fail to wait for God.

The second reason women can become an easy target is because of finances. I remember asking for help to pay my bills. Please understand that nothing is free. I have heard men say, "You weren't going to sleep with me" and "I'll call you later" as a way to keep me captive to what they wanted me to do. Sometimes, we tend to sell ourselves in some form or fashion. Now, when I need help paying my bills, I remember the promises that my Heavenly Father established for me. "But my God shall supply all your need according to his riches in glory by Christ Jesus" Philippians 4:19 (KJV). There are other distractions such as television, and let's not forget the saying "I am getting old." People sometimes think, *I am tired of being by myself or I want a family.* I recall our Heavenly Father said that we are never alone according to Hebrews 13:5 (NKJV), which says, "Let your conduct be without covetousness; be content with such things as you have. For He himself has said, 'I will never leave you nor forsake you.'" That means that we are never alone.

Let's keep in mind that we all have the same 12 emotions (fear, anxiety, shame, loneliness, stress, anger, depression, guilt, prejudice/false pride, trapped, betrayed, worthless).

Therefore, the only thing that would separate us is our decisions. We should be set apart and wait on Daddy.

Last but not at all least, we are easily distracted because we long for attention. Many people suffer from low self-esteem, which causes them to settle for any form of chaos in their life. I remember dating Kevin, who was open about how he felt about beautiful women. Kevin had a way of thinking that was not at all ideal to me.

His thought process said that if he was showing me a good time, I shouldn't complain about anything. I began to play the game with him and went with the flow of things because I didn't want to be single. The enemy was attempting to make me believe "I don't care how he treats me just as long as I have a man." Maybe someone can relate to this unhealthy way of thinking. I would say things like, "It took me too long to get him and I am not letting him go." We must keep in mind that the enemy comes to kill, steal, and destroy us. "The thief does not come except to steal, and to kill, and to destroy. I have come that they may have life, and that they may have it more abundantly" John 10:10 (NKJV). The adversary wants you to take your eyes off God and focus them on your situation. Let's be clear about something: Anything that stops you from living a God-purposed life is your adversary. God's blessings come without sorrow. Proverbs 10: 22 (NKJV) says, "The blessing of the Lord makes one rich, and He adds no sorrow with it." Once we become serious about what God has called us to do, we will be put to the test within our minds. We must take the time to study our opponent and discern good from evil. John the evangelist gave us instructions in 1 John 4:1 (NKJV): "Beloved, do not believe every spirit, but test the spirits, whether they are of God; because many false prophets have gone out into the world." That statement applies to both men and women.

It is important to pay close attention to our surroundings even within the place of worship. That means that every person who enters those doors is not your spouse, your baby's new daddy or someone to kick it with. Everyone who attends church or the assembly to worship does not have good intentions. There are a few that were sent (assignment) to steal you from God. This may be a surprise to you but there are some strong Bible-believing brothers who are struggling in their flesh and may use the word of God to get you into bed. You might get lucky when you tell him no and he cuts you off. It is important to study God's word for yourself to avoid being manipulated. Don't get caught up; some people live their lives saying "yes" to Jesus and saying "yes" to the world. Remember the old saying, "You can't have your cake and eat it too."

I remember being in a relationship with Sam, who I knew was cheating. I found a piece of paper with a woman's name, job, and home phone number. He really wanted to talk to her. At that time, there were no pagers or cellular phones, so we used pen and paper. I looked at the phone number and put it back in his pocket. When he woke up, he gave me a birthday card with money in it. I didn't mention the phone number because after work I was going shopping to buy myself a black leather coat. I didn't say anything. Like some of you, I was afraid that if he got mad, he would leave. I was not serving my heavenly Father at the time and as a result, I settled for a leather coat instead of speaking my mind.

In the winter of 1995, I told Barbara, my mother, that I was going to church with her. I would say that men made me run to Jesus. The icing on the cake was my son Steve. Steve had started experiencing his rebellious teen years. I was scared to do drugs and I didn't like to drink so I figured I would go to church for peace of mind. It's sad to say that I have never experienced a faithful relationship and I am almost 54 years old. That is crazy. Some people find it difficult to accept a person that is set apart and will not settle for nonsense. Healthy and faithful relationships do exist. While I'm waiting, I will let Dad (Jesus) heal my brokenness, rejection, and disappointments. Being in the mindset that said I must have someone no matter the cost had me frozen. The main reason I was frozen was because I did not have an earthly father in my life. I had no one to protect me or to talk to me about boys that become men and what they want.

When we do not know who we are and who we belong to, we will sometimes allow the enemy to destroy our soul. When you are mistreated for so long, you can become accustomed to being treated wrong. You tell yourself things like, "Well, we have been together for two or three years or even longer," and you start making excuses for behaviors that you wouldn't otherwise accept. We all can relate to loving someone to a fault. As I think back, that was the craziest thing I have ever heard. *I love you because you are mistreating me.* Let us expose the adversary. If you are not married, you are single, as mentioned in Ephesians 5:5 which says, "For this you know, that no fornicator, un-clean person, nor covetous man, who is an idolater, has any inheritance in the kingdom of Christ and God."

Believe it or not, the way you and I live does affect our family. The younger generation is being raised without knowing how a man or woman is supposed to treat them. They see how we are being mistreated so they begin to experience the very same thing and think it is acceptable. Their response could be, "How can you tell me what to do if you are not trying to correct your own relationship?" We influence our young women to live with men because they are only imitating us.

The younger generation are living together and using titles such as 'my fiancé' or 'my husband' with no plans on getting married. At this point, some of them have crossed the line by exchanging their personal information with one another. A person could be buying a car for their mate or sharing a bank account with the intention of never getting married. We consistently reap the benefits of being married without ever actually getting married. Hang in there. If you desire to be in a healthy and faithful relationship, do not be weary in well-doing for in due season we shall reap, if we faint not.

## *Chapter 2*
# CROSSING THE LINE

I had come to a point in my life that I trusted God with everything in my life except my relationships with men. Why? Because I did not know how to trust Him. I have always been in unfaithful relationships, so there were times that I figured I would help God out. Some women can cross the line when God tells us or shows us that someone is our mate. We begin to think to ourselves, *since he is the one it is okay to be intimate.* A little kissing and grinding should be okay. A big lie we tell ourselves is that since we are going to be married it's okay to sleep with our partner. We do it one time just to see if they will satisfy us physically. We tend to think things like, *I don't want to be stuck with them for the rest of my life and they don't know how to make love to me.*

We can't afford to play those games. There are some men who will not accept us teasing them and then saying, "No, I can't." It is very easy to cross the line when we are lonely. That's an open door to cross the line because your hormones are talking to you. Ladies especially experience this when their menstrual cycle is on or just went off. When we cross the line, it always causes separation between us and God. There is no person on earth worth losing your soul for. Prematurely telling a man too much information about yourself is crossing the line. Some people are quick to tell everything about themselves, thinking that they are just laying the cards on the table. We are too fast for our own good. Our heavenly Father gave us wisdom for every situation according to Colossians 1:9 (KJV), "For this cause we also, since the day we heard it, do not cease to pray for you, and to desire that ye might be filled with the knowledge of his will in all wisdom and spiritual understanding."

Once you have crossed the line, it causes you to lose your character and then sin starts out small and before you know it, we have been swallowed up. Christian single women cross the line when they are flirting with their sister's husband in the body of Christ. You know that you have crossed the line when you are including yourself in your girlfriend and her spouse's plans or steal your girlfriend's man because you think that the grass is greener on the other side. All relationships are tried in the fire.

Only God has the answer; just stand or sit still and listen. Hebrews 12:2 (NKJV) says, "Looking unto Jesus, the author and finisher of our faith, who for the joy that was set before Him endured the cross, despising the shame, and has sat down at the right hand of the throne of God." We can lose a good friend by crossing the line and putting them in harm's way because of our insecurities. Some people get mad when their plan doesn't work out. They find fault with the man by degrading him, such as name-calling. Have you heard someone say, "He is gay" because they were rejected? Let's be honest, no person wants to hear the word "no" when they want something. Hearing the word "no" is a challenge for us, and that rejection will drive us down the wrong road. Rejection makes the game more exciting to us because we won't stop until we have gotten him or her back in our lives.

Now he is tired of running and tired of telling you "no," so he gives in to you. The moment the intimacy is over, you feel guilty. You can't look one another in the face. You have destroyed a perfectly good friendship all because of not wanting to hear the two-letter word "no". Now, your friend doesn't call you and you are trying to figure out what's wrong with them. Sometimes we are never satisfied. Ecclesiastes 1:8 says, "All things are full of labor; man cannot express it. The eye is not satisfied with seeing, nor the ear filled with hearing." You can learn from the experience or continue to play games with your emotions and blame others. A person could be like a light switch; when the light goes out it is over. There is nothing you or I can do to change a person's mind. It makes no sense saying, "I will get him back."

When all else fails, we will contact our ex-boyfriend or our ex-girlfriend, forgetting the reason that they are an ex from the beginning.

Satan will tell you, "At least you are not by yourself." Another sign that we have not learned anything from our experiences is getting other people involved in getting them back. How many heartbreaks will it take for us to learn to let our heavenly Father send the right person for us? There is a purpose for the marriage and not just for the intimacy in the relationship. Singleness becomes peaceful when you admit that it is okay to be alone. Furthermore, there is the confidence that Jesus is always with us and we're never alone.

In the Bible, there are two words that describe a male and female relationship, betrothal, and marriage. You are either engaged or you are married. There is not an in-between. Let's not cross the line, ladies and gentlemen. We should aim to be like our sister in Ruth 2:4-10. We must be busy for God by helping to build His kingdom. Luke 2:49 (NKJV) says, "And He said to them, 'Why did you seek me? Did you not know that I must be about my Father's business?'" Boaz will notice us working in the kingdom and come and sweep us off our feet.

*Chapter 3*

# THE DANGER OF CROSSING THE LINE IN THE SPIRIT REALM:
*Transferring Spirits through the Hymen*

Count the cost when you cross the line and sleep with a man before marriage, especially if you are not equally yoked. I look at unequally yoked as not being on the same page concerning what you both want out of life. Keep in mind that marriage is for a purpose and that is to help build the kingdom of God. Do you both have the same vision, beliefs, and desires? Who would be paying the household bills? Will he be the sole provider, or would you be contributing to the finances? Ask questions and don't compromise if you don't like what you are hearing. Do not turn a deaf ear if you were told by your Heavenly Father that he is not the one. Let's define danger. Danger can be seen or unseen trouble such as getting pregnant, receiving a sexually transmitted disease or baby mama drama.

When we sleep with someone before marriage, we give them a part of ourselves. I can hear you saying, "How is that possible?" I am glad that you asked. When men and women exchange sexual organisms, you are exchanging with each other your very beings. You are giving that person everything that you've got in your body, mind, and soul. Now hear this everyone, at this point you will be held accountable for what you know. Repent and lay aside every sin that easily ensnares you (Romans 12:1).

If we are sincere about our repentance, as stated in 1 Corinthians 10:12-13 (NKJV), "Therefore, let him who thinks he stands take heed lest he fall. No temptation has overtaken you except such as is common to man: but God is faithful who will not allow you to be tempted beyond what you are able, but with the temptation will also make a way of escape that you may be able to bear it." It is plain and simple: We must decide to repent and turn from our wicked ways.

We transfer spirits when we have intercourse. Have you noticed that once you break up with someone, they still want to be with you? Or maybe you want them, no matter how badly they have treated you. Having sex before marriage opens a door that only God can close. Genesis 4:7 (NKJV) says, "If you do well, will you not be accepted? And if you do not do well, sin lies at the door. And its desire is for you, but you should rule over it."

You should know about the female reproductive system. We are going to discuss the female hymen. Waiting until you are married to have sex could save you from heartaches. The hymen is located outside of the vagina. The hymen is named after the Greek God Hymenaeus, the God of marriage and wedding. The dictionary defines the hymen as a layer of tissue; it's a mucous membrane that is part of the genital organs. The hymen is a covering; you are a virgin until the hymen has been broken. That's why there is a sign of blood on your first sexual encounter.

The danger is once you both have climaxed and exchange fluids, you are now one. Can you see the big picture? When we sleep with someone we are walking away with a part of that person's bodily fluids in us. Just the thought scares me, especially if they are sexually active. Let's not be like the Samaritan woman who had five husbands and wasn't married to any one of them (John 4: 16-18). To my sisters and brothers, we can live again just as the Samaritan woman did when she admitted her current position in life. We must acknowledge that looking for love in a man or woman can't fill that void that only God can fill. The Samaritan woman had no clue that she would be filled with the living water that flows freely from Jesus. We shall thirst no more because the void has been filled. Do you want to be bound or free?

*Chapter 4*

# THE MISCARRIAGE:
## *Aborting the Baby (God's Vision)*

To miscarry means to not develop to full term or reach the result. I can see miscarriage in two ways. The first way is a natural fetus and the second is a spiritual fetus. Let's talk about the fetus. We can lose a baby through no fault of our own. It could be health reasons that caused complications. We could also choose to abort the baby by having an abortion or not following the doctor's orders. Spiritual miscarriage is when you or I run from God and become disobedient. We start doing our own thing. Satan has an assignment for each of us to abort God's vision for our lives.

The enemy will tell you, "You have already done it, so why stop?" He will lie and say, "God doesn't care, and He is not going to forgive you." We all know that Satan is the father of all lies. If Eve was deceived, brothers and sisters, we are not exempt. The opposite sex wants to convince us that if we only have sex once everything will be okay, but there are consequences for every action. I remember Romans 12:1-2 (NKJV) saying, "I beseech you therefore, brethren, by the mercies of God, that you present your bodies a living sacrifice, holy and acceptable to God, which is your reasonable service. And do not be conformed to this world, but be transformed by the renewing of your mind, that you may prove what is that good and acceptable and perfect will of God."

Please be very careful because Satan will use your close friends to entice you. Examine your friendships with the opposite sex. We are quick to call a friend our brother or sister in the Lord. What is wrong with us? Have you examined why you call him brother? Do you see him as your brother or someone you have a crush on? James 1:14 (NKJV) tells us, "But each one is tempted when he is drawn away by his own desires and enticed." We have Jesus telling us how to live, then we have Satan telling us how we should live. Then we give power to other people telling us how we should live. Here is the kicker: We tell ourselves how we should live. We have these voices telling us what to do. The question is how do I learn to hear God's voice and block out Satan and friends? Our instructions are in II Chronicles 7: 14 (NKJV), which states, "If My people who are called by My name will humble themselves, and pray and seek My face, and turn from their wicked ways, then I will hear from heaven, and will forgive their sin and heal their land." That is a promise from our Heavenly Father.

God has given each of us spiritual gifts to use for the body and to help build His kingdom (I Corinthians 12: 1-11). Brothers and sisters, know that you have power from on high and Satan wants to take it from you. Just think of how you would feel if someone visited you and they began to make changes in your house without asking. How would you feel? The same thing happens when we let Satan in our lives: He comes in and rearranges the furniture without asking. Write God's vision in your heart and stay focused. Habakkuk 2:2 (NKJV) says, "Then the Lord answered me and said: Write the vision and make it plain on tablets, that he may run who reads it." Seek God for your ministry. If you know your ministry, it is time to get back on post.

There are two types of singleness. The first is holding on to someone that we can go back to instead of being by ourselves. That is called having an emotional tie. We all have someone that we can go back to. First ask yourselves if it is worth the pain and agony. The second form of singleness is having no attachment emotionally to anyone but God. Single couples, saved and un-saved, tend to do everything together like a married couple. If you open a bank account with someone, you've now exposed your personal information to someone that you may not be with. Bank accounts, house keys, going on nice vacations, and buying big gifts for each other are reminiscent of what married people do. Now, if you get married, you'll have run out of ideas for things to do with your spouse. You are bored with the person you chose to live your life with. I remember my friend John telling me that "sin makes you stupid." People have unprotected sex and then become afraid that they might be pregnant. Once the woman finds out that she is fine, she does it all over again.

Our lives are like a parking garage. We are the cars and God is the driver. We drive into the parking garage, get our ticket which is the word of God, then look for a parking spot. There are several levels in God. We keep going until we find a location. We park our cars and get out to do our thing. It's time to return to our cars to avoid paying extra time on the meter. As we are leaving the parking garage there are arrows pointing to the exit sign, but we see a shorter way out. We continue to drive and end up at a dead end. Do you turn the car around or overlook the dead-end sign and continue to drive the wrong way? You pass the rails and get four flat tires. There are different levels of sin. Sin takes us off course and leads us to dead ends. This often takes longer than we intended. Sometimes we don't make it back to the driver (God). God is always there to give us directions. John 10: 27 (KJV) says, "My sheep hear my voice, and I know them, and they follow me."

*Chapter 5*

# WILL YOU BE MADE WHOLE?

Do you want to be made whole? John 5:6 (NKJV) says, "When Jesus saw him lying there, and knew that he already had been in that condition a long time, He said to him, "Do you want to be made well?"

I remember thinking about the question Jesus asked the man at the pool. There were several sick people hanging around the pool. Some were blind, lame, and paralyzed waiting for the moving of the water. If we aren't careful, we can become just like the sick people by the pool, waiting for someone else to help us. There are some people hanging out at the pool just for fun; nothing is wrong with them. They are just watching and being in everybody else's business. Life experiences should not paralyze our minds and have us looking to everyone for help. There are times that we may be in this mindset and may be totally silent and can't open our mouths while reaching out for help.

Our friends and family walk by, not knowing that we are trapped. Now, do you want to be made whole? God can ease our pain when we have intimacy with Him. God will not use us and then walk away. Only God can move us from the pool. Once we accept Jesus as our personal savior, we shall be saved. Romans 10:9 says, "If you confess with your mouth the Lord Jesus and believe in your heart that God has raised Him from the dead, you will be saved." We are no longer in darkness to the schemes of the enemy, no longer paralyzed in our minds/thoughts.

We are free because Jesus meets us right where we are in our lives, just like Jesus met the Samaritan woman (John 4:17-18) at the well and exposed her way of living. She was trapped looking for love in a man until she'd drawn water from the only man that could quench her thirst. The Samaritan woman will never thirst again (John 4:14). To become whole, first we must admit where we are in our lives. Jesus wants to have a relationship with His sons and daughters.

Jesus is our physician (Matthew 9:12). Mark 2:17 (NKJV) says, "When Jesus heard it, He said to them, 'Those who are well have no need of a physician.'" It is by Jesus that the world is healed of their sins; it was by His stripes that we are healed. That means we do not have an excuse to stay in any unhealthy relationships. I remember relationships being the hardest thing to let go of and give to God. I didn't trust God to handle my relationships with men. God said to me, "You keep picking the men because you don't trust me." It took another unfaithful relationship for me to finally get it. I overcame my fear of trusting God when I stopped looking at Him as a man. I began to see Him through another pair of lenses as my spiritual father and not an earthly father. See, my earthly father lied to me and abandoned me.

My father abandoned me when I was two years old. He married another woman and started a family. In August of 2003, I met my father for the first time at the age of 30. We kept in touch for a couple of months. Then I was right back where I started, feeling rejected. He stopped calling and wouldn't return my phone calls. Can you relate to why I couldn't trust God in the beginning? The key to my healing was praying and being honest with God about how I felt about being abandoned, rejected, and overlooked by the man that was supposed to protect me. God said, "Joanne, I did not allow you to die mentally. I was still there protecting you."

To be made whole, we as women must let go of the world's way of thinking. You must know who you are and really believe it. Relationships come and go but Jesus will always be with us. The key is to let Him work in us and on us. Are you ready for love? People are so broken on the inside. Only God can heal our heart without leaving a scar. If we want to be made whole, it is our responsibility to live our lives according to the word of God. It will require for us to be naked and not ashamed before Him. We must accept who we are and where we are emotionally in our life. To avoid walking through revolving doors, you must change your mindset about yourself and life around you. Don't lie around at the pool and miss out on what God has for you.

Our first love is Jesus. Therefore, He has the plan for our lives. To know the will of God we must pray (communicate, talk) to Him. Healing requires sanctification, renewing of your mind. Romans 12:1-2 (NKJV) says, "I beseech you therefore, brethren, by the mercies of God, that you present your bodies a living sacrifice, Holy and acceptable to God, which is your reasonable service. And do not be conformed to this world, but be transformed by the renewing of your mind, that you may prove what is that good and acceptable and perfect will of God." That means when relationships go wrong, do not run right into another man's arms. The only thing you are doing is running from yourself. Take time out to see what is really going on. Most of the time, our decisions stem from our childhood and are carried right into adulthood. There comes a time that we must take ownership of our lives and stop blaming others. All living things need love to grow. God gives us nutrients through His love, which is the word of the Bible. Everything we need is right in Him. We must ask for it.

I realized that I was made whole once I discovered how to love myself. Everyone wants to be loved. It is so important to love yourself first, just in case no one will ever tell you that they love you. When it comes to loving someone else, we must wait on God (Dad) to show us who the person is. A broken heart that does not trust will bring their hurt and pain right into a relationship and mess things up. Let God heal you and send the mate that was selected for you. Do you remember Abraham selected a bride for his son Isaac in Genesis 24:24?

Love is like baking a cake. Psalm 34:8 (NKJV) says, "Oh, taste and see that God is good." I can wait with patience until the cake is done or I can throw the cake away because it was half-baked. When we throw the cake away, it is because of not having faith or patience. We walk away. Taking the cake out of the oven too soon can cause unnecessary hurt and pain because we want a spouse now. We can put the cake back in the oven and let it continue to bake and wait for the finished product. No one wants to be a pretty cake with icing on the outside and messed up on the inside. The desire is to be a pretty cake that is well done. There is no relationship that can compare to our relationship with God. Scripturally, you are already a bride unto Jesus, and He is your groom. It is impossible to have a healthy relationship on Earth if you do not have a relationship with God. Jesus is our groom who we are to love and respect always and not just when things are going well in our life.

What are the responsibilities of a groom? A groom is to show you another level in love. He is intimate with you, and you tell him everything. The groom has some of the same responsibilities as our Heavenly Father. The groom must take care of us and always have our best interest. One night in prayer, I saw a vision of me walking down a church aisle to get married. Before I could get to the groom, I opened my eyes and began to cry. I cried because I didn't want God, my heavenly father, to leave me. I could see not having my free time with Him. I thought that when I got married, He was going to leave me. The Holy Spirit began to calm me down and ask me, "Joanne, where is the bride's father standing?" I responded, "He is standing right there beside me." While I was still crying, God said, "Yes, he is still your father and he is turning you over to a man that will make you happy."

The Father (God) is standing right there whenever we need Him. God will always be our father and He is not going to leave us. God told me, "There are some things I want you to have, but you only can receive them if you are married." I responded, "I do not know how to be a bride." The Holy Spirit said, "I will teach you." That was an eye-opener for me. I do not know how to be a bride in the spirit realm, so I have to say that I am not ready to be an earthly bride. Hearing myself saying that took away my anxiety at getting married. First, I want to be a perfect bride unto Jesus. This was awesome. The Holy Spirit said, "A bride is looking forward to the preparation to see the groom." Do you remember what queen Esther's 12 months of preparation was like? Six months with oil of myrrh and six months with perfumes (Esther 2: 12). It is simple. We must be happy with ourselves before we can make someone else happy.

Hosea and Gomer are good examples of true love. Hosea's name means deliver. Gomer's name means complete (a picture of Israel being brought back to God). Gomer was not complete until she was delivered back into the hands of her husband. Hosea 3:3 (KJV) says,

"And I said unto her, 'Thou shalt abide for me many days; thou shalt not play the harlot, and thou shalt not be for another man: so will I also be for thee.'" Ephesians 5:25 (KJV) says, "Husbands love your wives, even as Christ also loved the church, and gave himself for it." Yes, we are chosen brides. We must give Jesus our consent like Rebecca gave her consent to Elizer, Abraham's servant.

Let's talk about Rebecca. Genesis 24:58 (KJV) says, "And they called Rebekah, and said unto her, 'Wilt thou go with this man?' And she said, 'I will go.'" As brides we receive gifts from the Holy Spirit which are spiritual. James stated, "Every good gift and every perfect gift is from above, and cometh down from the Father of lights, with whom is no variableness, neither shadow of turning" James 1:17 (KJV). Hear me loud and clear: There were no couples that dated and lived together before getting married in the Bible. There are two words, betrothed, meaning engaged, or you were married. So we are going to be the five wise virgins who were ready when Jesus the bridegroom came and those who were ready went in with Him to the wedding. Read Matthew 25: 1-10 for a better understanding of this. Our honeymoon will be the time of intimacy with Jesus. 1 Peter 1:15 (NKJV) says, "but as He who called you is holy, you also be holy in all your conduct." You now may kiss the bride.

## Chapter 6
# WHO AM I?

The Bible says that I am a jewel (Isaiah 61:10). I am a precious diamond to Daddy. This diamond in the rough is called Joanne. A diamond that was lost, broken, and needed repair. A diamond that was unpolished in the mine. Covered in dust with sharp edges and no one to trust. Surrounded with different types of specimens (men) with different qualities. A diamond that has no color because of a loose heart looking for love. Until, one day a special hand prepared a way for me. Even though I was pressed down in the rough, God saw that I was unique and precious in His sight. I am no longer that diamond called Joanne. My name has been changed. I am now a gem because God paid the price for me.

We are of great value to Jesus. He tells us that we are the apple of His eye. Deuteronomy 32:10 (NKJV) says, "He found him in a desert land and in the wasteland, a howling wilderness; He encircled him, He instructed him, He kept him as the apple of His eye." Through all my wrong decisions in relationships, God was always there. When I thought that no one (a man) loved me I was always an apple in my Daddy's eyes. God said before I was formed in my mother's womb, He knew me. Jeremiah stated, "Before I formed you in the womb I knew you; I sanctified you; I ordained you a prophet to the nations." Jeremiah 1:5 (NKJV).

Are you hearing what is being said? God took His time and fearfully and wonderfully made you and me. Psalm 139:14 (NKJV) says, "I will praise you, for I am fearfully and wonderfully made, marvelous are your works, and that my soul knows very well." God is awesome. It took me a long time to get it in my head and heart that as a single woman I can be set apart. I had to learn my own self-value. I know that my life is not my own. We all are given instructions to carry out for the Lord. I am on a journey passing through, but the revelation is I don't know where I am going. Since I am on a journey without knowing where I am going, I am not lost because God is my compass. The next revelation is I must stay close to Daddy, so I will not get lost. In the natural world, I am not good with directions. I can get lost easily. I am not gifted in that area, so my family and friends have to provide me with landmarks when giving me directions. My mother would spend her day off from work going places with me so that I could get to my destinations. Barbara would say, "Joanne, stop planning my days for me."

Can you imagine my Heavenly Father and me walking down the street together in New York City, and because of the population I am holding His hand real tight. I am walking close to Him, so close that no one can walk between Him and me. I will stop when He stops and walk when He walks. I will not get excited and let his hands go and run off.

I must stay close. "I am the true vine, and My Father is the vinedresser. Every branch in Me that does not bear fruit He takes away; and every branch that bears fruit He prunes, that it may bear more fruit. You are already clean because of the word which I have spoken to you. Abide in Me, and I in you. As the branch cannot bear fruit of itself, unless it abides in the vine, neither can you, unless it abides in the vine, neither can you, unless you abide in Me" John

15:1, 4 (NKJV). Picture a forest. All forests have a trail that leads you from start to finish. Going through the forest, you must stay focused on the trail. In the forest are many distractions, such as little bugs, worms, snakes, and deer. Do you get the picture? It may rain, snow and sleet but you must keep going until you reach the end of the forest. The only way you will find out who you are is by staying connected to the vine which is your creator. There are no shortcuts. Psalm 1:3 (NKJV) says, "He shall be like a tree planted by the rivers of water, that bring forth his fruit in its season, whose leaf also shall not wither, and whatever he does shall prosper."

There is no ending to finding out who you are. You might have to trace back your ancestry to find out why you act a certain way. I have the traits of my grandmother Mary McCrae, who was a strong woman. She moved north with her husband and three children. She kept a clean house and loved to cook. My mother Barbara taught me wisdom about life and didn't hold back the truth concerning life. I remember my grandmother and mother made sure that I behaved like a young lady growing up. I have three brothers, Gregory, Fred, and Shelton; my sister Katerry came along years later. My grandmother would come to the front door and call me over to her and say, "Joanne, stop that running up and down the streets with those boys or I will make you come in the house." I would sit on the steps and watch my brothers play or I would play with my doll baby. I discovered years later that both of my great grandparents were Native Americans. Who am I? I came from two different cultures, African American and Native American. Let's not forget my own way of thinking called character.

Who am I? I am a single African American woman who must be about the concerns of my heavenly father as stated in 1 Corinthians 7:34 (KJV), "There is a difference between a wife and a virgin. The unmarried woman careth for the things of the Lord, that she may be holy both in body and in spirit: but she that is married careth for the things of the world, how she may please her husband." I now understand. And He said to them, "Why did you seek Me? Did you not know that I must be about my Father's business?" Luke 2:49 (NKJV)

Who am I? I am my Heavenly Father's daughter who is called to serve others. I am a servant; it is important that we know who we are to avoid pain of seeking validation from others. Know your self-worth and be comfortable with your body. Don't let anyone tell you who you are. If you have questions about who you are, go to the creator who made you. Stay connected.

## Chapter 7

# WHEN YOU THINK HE'S THE RIGHT ONE

Here is a big question that we ask God: "Is he or she the right one?" Listen, he or she could be the right one, but it would require being obedient from both parties. God sent an angel to Mary and then to Joseph to confirm what was said. God will speak to both parties in His time. God may tell one so that person will have patience with the other person. When the Lord tells you that he or she is the one, and one day things are going fine, then the person acts like they are not interested in you, what do you do? Remember you said Jesus said that they were your spouse. What do you do when you are getting tired and want to throw in the towel? You have spent time, maybe years, with the person. Everything feels right and looks right but he's not ready to commit to you. What do you do when Jesus says, "Yes, I sent him or her into your life?" You may say, "Jesus if you sent him/her, what is wrong? Why are things so crazy?" Have you experienced feeling alone in the relationship but holding on because Jesus said He sent them? Let's keep in mind that God is a good father. He wants nothing but the best for his children.

Dad said, "If you then, being evil, know how to give good gifts to your children, how much more will your father who is in heaven give good things to those who ask Him!" Matthew 7:11 (NKJV). When it comes to relationships there is no manual to buy from the newsstand, bookstore, or online. We are offered several help books but not a step-by-step manual to help us when needed. God is the manual that we need, and it requires us to listen and obey His instructions. There is no perfect relationship; we must speak God's word to the situation if we want to see a change. All relationships are tried by fire and if you gave your all and were obedient to the Lord, it will work for your good.

Jesus' patience is not like man's but let me tell you God's patience does run out. I was in a relationship with Bob and spent more time alone than with him. I was holding on to God's word that He spoke to me concerning him. The Lord coached me through and kept saying, "Trust Me." Well, as time went on Bob and I spent less time with each other. We began to drift apart and the next thing I knew he was telling me that he was not ready to be in a relationship with me. We dated for two years without being intimate with each other. He respected me being born again and never crossed the line with me, so we ended up being close friends.

I asked God (DAD) what happened, and He responded, "Joanne his time has run out and I cannot prolong my promise to you." God our Father does see what is going on with us. I met a nice gentleman named John while attending a theological school; he was in my class. One evening, he called asking me about an assignment that was due, and we discussed it together. A couple of days later my niece said, "Aunt Joanne, call John" and I was puzzled and asked her why. John had called my niece and left a message with her for me to contact him. I returned his call and he asked me out for lunch, and I agreed.

We became friends and began hanging out more. John asked me if I would go to church with him. John was active in his congregation: a deacon, a musician, and he often worked with children's church. One day, he caught me off guard and asked if we could be a couple. It scared me at first because I had become comfortable with being single. I said, "Yes," and this is what happens when you think that he is the right one. I met his son, who was six years old at the time, and then his family. I was introduced to his parents and siblings and attended every family function. Time went by so fast. We dated for a year. Take note that I said, "we dated." We were not in a relationship. In my opinion, a relationship consists of sleeping together.

Hold on to your seat. His pattern began to change. He was calling me less and was working more on the weekend. I had been disappointed so much with men that I knew the signs of unfaithfulness. I received a phone call while driving home from work one evening. I thought the call was to discuss which movie we were going to see. Tuesday nights were movie night for us at Franklin Mills Mall.

Two days before our first anniversary, he called and told me that he had not been faithful and broke it off with me. I was speechless and hung up on him. I was upset because John approached me and asked if we could be a couple. I was so close to having the man that I had desired, but I had to look at the blessing. He and I were not intimate, which made it so easy to get over him.

God had done something that was puzzling. He said, "Joanne, call him back and tell him that you forgive him." I sat at my desk crying and telling the Lord (DAD), "He cheated on me and You want me to call him back to tell him that I forgive him?" I was totally against it; I said, "No God, not this time. I am sorry, and I will take the punishment for being disobedient to you." It took me an hour and a half to pick up the telephone and call John, who hurt me, and say, "I forgive you." My forgiveness toward him left him speechless, he didn't say a word after I spoke. John and I remained friends and kept in contact with one another, practically phone pals. Eventually we both stopped calling and eight months later I found out through his parents that he got married. He met someone online and instantly married her; I was detached from him; therefore, I wasn't upset about the news.

My Heavenly Father said, "Since you kept my word and you were obedient and kept yourself, which is honorable to me, I will reward you openly." God will honor me for being honorable unto Him. I found favor in God's sight, so my brother and sister, when you think that he/she is the right one and it doesn't work out, don't lose sight of your first love. Your priority is loving yourself. Remember you are now whole in God and he saves the best for last.

The desire I have in my heart is from God and one day I will be happily married to a man who loves me. "Delight yourself also in the Lord, and He shall give you the desires of your heart." Psalm 37: 4 (NKJV). Do not give up.

## Chapter 8
# SO CLOSE BUT NOT YET

Have you ever wanted something badly and once you received it, it did not feel real? God is a good "God" and He knows what and who is best for us. Life will challenge us, and the question would be are we paying attention? Often, our human nature says, "I can handle anything that comes my way." We know as children of the Lord that we can't do anything in our own strength. "The Lord is my light and my salvation; whom shall I fear? The Lord is the strength of my life; of whom shall I be afraid?" Psalm 27:1 (KJV)

I was forced to take a stand for myself or go into a marriage knowing that Wade was not right for me. I refused to marry someone just to have their last name. I was so close to saying "I do" but called the wedding off a couple of months before. How do you handle life when you both start out loving Jesus together then one of you takes your eyes off Jesus and leaves the other standing in the wilderness? My wilderness was having a wedding dress; my maid of honor and flower girl had their dresses.

The day I selected my wedding invitations, I heard a small voice talking to me. The small voice said, "Not yet, wait" and the other voice said, "But you are so close; just keep going." Praise God because He knows the future. We can only see what is in front of us.

It is funny that sometimes we can't see what's in front of us for many reasons. My wilderness was to be so close to having the man I had dreamed of, someone to love me and spoil me with attention.

My wilderness left me feeling numb and emotionless even though it was my call. I called the wedding off. I was saying to myself, *how can Wade decide to follow another voice when he knows Jesus' voice?* "My sheep hear my voice and I know them, and they follow me." John 10:27 (KJV) As I have stated earlier in the book, my relationships always end with an unfaithful companion. This time the unfaithfulness was to an addiction. I felt like the addiction was the other woman because I was put second again. I was familiar with a cheating boyfriend but never anyone who had a drug addiction. I noticed that Wade's behavior had begun to change. We had less communication between us, less Sunday service, and he always had an excuse why he could not see me. My dry desert (wilderness) made it hard to handle or even accept Wade with his addiction. We are given a choice in life, to be happy or to settle. John says, "The thief does not come except to steal, and to kill, and to destroy. I have come that they may have life, and that they may have it more abundantly." John 10:10 (NKJV)

I like the way the Message Bible says it: "I came so they can have real and external life, more and better life than they ever dreamed of" John 10:10. We are not to be ignorant of Satan's devices. I asked myself, *Will I choose life and have it abundantly or will I choose death and reap the hardship for being disobedient to the Lord?* God gives us free will. Once we are shown the truth, we cannot close our eyes or ears and walk around like nothing is wrong. It is simple: Do not ignore the red flags. Deuteronomy 30:19 (NKJV) says, "I call heaven and earth as witness today against you, that I have set before you life and death, blessings and cursing; therefore choose life, that both you and your descendants may live."

The wilderness experience made me withdraw from my family and friends, and I could not pray. I could not cry or even talk about it. I was **ANGRY** at Wade because he said he loved me, and I believed him. I never thought that I would say, "I am not praying for him." For my healing to begin, I had to admit that I was hurt and disappointed, and that I contributed to my own pain. I did not wait on God. I had to rely on the Lord for strength and to mend my broken heart. Timothy 2:13 (NKJV) says, "If we are faithless, He remains faithful; He cannot deny Himself."

I belong to Him and God (Dad) will not deny me His healing power. God said, He will never leave you nor forsake you, according to Hebrews 13:5. In our wilderness, we gain strength to call on Jesus; now I can pray for Wade. I was blind Bartimaeus crying out to the Lord (Mark 10: 46-52).

You see the tares of this world are a part of our development of life (Matthew 13: 24-30). The seeds and tares must grow together to produce a good product for the Master. Every one of us has good seed in us because we are made in the image of Jesus. The enemy comes to sow tares in our lives but as we grow in the Lord, we sprout and produce a good crop. I said all that to say that our wilderness is a part of our walk with God. I will wear a new wedding dress at the appointed time. The old wedding dress is still hanging in my sister's closet.

"You will keep him in perfect peace, whose mind is stayed on You, because he trusts in You. Trust in the Lord forever, For in Yah, the Lord, is everlasting strength." Isaiah 26: 3-4 (NKJV)

**AMEN**

*Chapter 9*

# MARRIAGE IS A COVENANT

So you are getting married? Let us talk about the word covenant. It means an agreement, or contract between two parties to do something specified. The Etymology dictionary explained it another way: "to come together, join, fit and suit." The covenant (agreement) will be our wedding vows. ***Do you promise to love, honor, and cherish for better or for worse, for richer or for poorer, in sickness and in health? And forsaking all others, will you remain only unto him/her for as long as you both shall live?*** The contract would be sealed with the words **"*I do.*"** The icing on the cake would be exchanging of rings: "***With this ring I pledge my love and commitment.***" The bride and groom seal the contract from God" "***You may kiss the bride.***"

Do not take the Lord's marriage contract lightly. Before you commit to one another seek wise counseling. Pray and ask the Holy Spirit for direction throughout the pre-marital period. If you want Jesus' blessings you must be obedient to Him. It is like asking our earthly father for his blessing and approval, and his opinion about the person that you have chosen to spend the rest of your life with. Your spiritual leader will counsel you together in several pre-marital sessions. The purpose of each session is to see if you both are ready to make a lifetime commitment.

Your leader has an obligation to God concerning your commitment to one another because you are making an oath before Him. A marriage covenant is between God and two people. "Then God saw everything that He had made, and indeed it was very good." Genesis 1:31 (NKJV). "So then, they are no longer two but one flesh. Therefore, what God has joined together, let not man separate." Matthew 19:6 (NKJV). That is deep. Do not let man separate you from your marriage. That means that you and I cannot let anything separate us from our spouse. Your marriage will go through tough times but remember your lifelong commitment. "My brethren, count it all joy when you fall into various trials," James 1:2 (NKJV). Let us trust in God and lay down our emotions, our will, and our expectations of how Jesus should do things.

## Chapter 10
# ARE YOU REALLY READY?

Ask yourself if you are ready to share yourself with another person. Am I ready to show all my flaws? Am I ready to receive his flaws? Am I ready to show him the other side, such as no makeup, not wearing pretty clothing, and let us not forget the closet filled with shoes? Hey, what about our bad hair days? Are we ready to show our true colors when it is that time of the month? Are we ready to share ourselves when we do not feel like talking and just want to relax and watch television? Are we ready when he or she wants our attention and at that moment we are not in the mood to be touched? Are we ready to show that we are not good cooks or show that we keep an unorganized house where only we know where something is? Are you ready to settle down and give up that female friend on the side? Are you ready to talk and listen even when you do not feel like it? Are you ready to give an account of your day without lying about your whereabouts? Men, are you ready to give up your mother for her? Are you ready to be a supporter by enhancing her life for the both of you? Are you ready to let your boys go and stop listening to opinions from those who are still single? Bonus question for everyone! Are you ready to serve the other person with a willing heart?

*Chapter 11*

# WHILE YOU ARE WAITING

While you are waiting be honest with yourself about your own feelings. Let us examine ourselves before moving forward. How do you feel about the person—look at the whole picture and do not leave anything out. Don't lie to yourself and say, "I am ok, I forgive them," but as soon as you hear their voice your attitude changes. Let us look at the meaning of examine according to Webster: "to inspect or scrutinize carefully; to observe, test or investigate, order to evaluate." Once we confess where we are with our emotions then we can move forward with our life. Psalm 26:2 (NKJV) says, "Examine me, O Lord, and prove me; try my mind and my heart." Seek God for your next direction and for your healing. Psalm 147:3 (NKJV) says, "He heals the brokenhearted and binds up their wounds."

Once you are healed and back on track then go and help someone else. Remember, we are that diamond in the rough that was polished to go to the nation and be a blessing. With the help of the Holy Spirit, we are going to polish every un-cut gem that we meet to let them know that they are not lost or forgotten. We know that they have been brought with a price.

*Chapter 12*

# STAYING FOCUSED

When we are focused our vision becomes clear. Staying focused allows Jesus to work in our lives. When we are focused it can prevent us from being hurt from relationships, no matter how long you have known them, no matter if he/she says that they love you. It could help to avoid a broken heart. If we wait for the Lord to send our mates, we can avoid broken promises. "Most men will proclaim each his own goodness, but who can find a faithful man?" Proverbs 20: 6 (NKJV)

We can learn to love ourselves when we are focused. Everyone desires to experience someone loving them. Ladies do not let your guard down. Set high standards when it comes to having sex, being intimate, making love, or just kicking it. I do not care how you try to cover it up. Do not settle for anyone mistreating you. Do not allow anyone to disrespect you. We can love ourselves. Staying focused means letting go of the past and opening your mind, body, and soul to Jesus. 1 Thessalonians 5:23 (NKJV) says, "Now may the God of peace Himself sanctify you completely and may your whole spirit, soul, and body be preserved blameless at the coming of our Lord Jesus Christ."

We will be kept if we stay focused, Our Heavenly Father is watching over his sons and daughters. John 17:12 (NKJV) says, "While I was with them in the world, I kept them in Your name. Those whom you gave Me I have kept; and none of them is lost except the son of perdition, that the Scripture might be fulfilled." King David assured us that we have nothing to fear because Jesus is with us. Psalm 23:4 (KJV) says, "Yea, though I walk through the valley of the shadow of death, I will fear no evil: for thou art with me; thy rod and thy staff they comfort me." Be true to yourself and do not let anyone move you from your current position: "to thine own self be true" (Polonius in *Hamlet*). I had to ask myself why I was here, why I was afraid to be by myself, why I allowed men to mistreat me. I had to change my thinking process according to II Corinthians 13:5 (NKJV), which says, "Examine yourselves as to whether you are in the faith. Test yourselves. Do you not know yourselves, that Jesus Christ is in you? Unless indeed you are disqualified." I had to recognize my error and forgive myself and others that had disappointed me, mishandled me, and lied to me.

Rest in the Lord and He will comfort you. Imagine yourself free and living the life you have always dreamed of. Run this race with a purpose by starting small as stated in Philippians 2:16 (NKJV), "Holding fast the word of life, so that I may rejoice in the day of Christ that I have not run in vain or labored in vain."

*Chapter 13*

# GOING TO THE NEXT LEVEL

I could not have reached the next level without removing the barriers in my life. As I put the pieces together, I was able to get to the root of my issues. Learning to love me while putting the pieces back together opened doors for deliverance. It required me to put away the foolish things according to 1 Corinthians 13: 11 (NKJV), "When I was a child, I spoke as a child, I understood as a child, I thought as a child; but when I became a man, I put away childish things." Like the prodigal son in Luke 15:17, I came to myself after trying to walk this journey without my Heavenly Father. I came to myself and realized that everything and everybody is not a part of the plan. Once I took my eyes off myself, then things began to fall into place.

Learning to love me required a real look in the mirror as to "why" I allowed certain things in my life. As I stated, "When I was a child, I thought as a child." As a child, I knew that my mom loved me, but what about my father who I didn't meet until I was 35 years old because of his wife. At that age, I had already made some bad decisions and accepted things that bought me pain. Not being loved by my father and not having him to contribute to my life are the reasons for me wanting to learn how to love myself.

How can I love myself when the person who bought me into this world was not a part of my life to show me what love was? When I came to myself, I understood that my father was not a bad person and I forgave him. In the year 2019, he and I reunited again and shortly after he was gone again. My father and I would talk twice a day, in the morning as I drove to work and in the evening on my way home from work. We talked for a month and a half, until his stepdaughter found out that I was calling him. I would call him because he could not see clearly to dial my phone number. His stepdaughter had his cellular phone number changed and would not give the number to her siblings to avoid me contacting him. I am fine knowing that my father asked me to come and stay with him for a week during my summer vacation. He stated, "Baby, Daddy got the money, so don't worry about anything." Our last conversation was in May 2019, as I walked away hearing words from him that I play over and over in my head. I can hear him saying, "How's my oldest baby girl doing? You know that your father loves you and no matter how old you are, sweetheart, you will always be my baby."

I also stopped trying to make love happen with men and learned how to be a friend without having any strings attached. Going to the next level meant that I stopped being fast and thinking that I knew what was best for me. I apologized to God for taking so long to trust Him. I had to break the cycle of looking for love so that I could live a healthy life. Once I forgave my father and myself, I was set free from the spirit of rejection.

I was paralyzed in my thinking, just like the paralytic man. Mark 2:3 (NKJV) says, "Then they came to Him, bringing a paralytic who was carried by four men." Going to the next level allowed me to set boundaries and hold people accountable for their actions. Doing so gave me a sense of freedom from within. Being happy from within is not based on things or a person. Learning to love me requires me to look for me, while putting the pieces of the puzzle together. I like the quote "Who in the world am I?" Ah, that's the great puzzle by Lewis Carroll.

Now that I can see the next level, a women's ministry has been birthed. I must protect the birth of the ministry until I receive further instructions from DAD. I now understand the scripture Romans: 8:28 (TLB), "And we know that all that happens to us is working for our good if we love God and are fitting into his plans." It's awesome to know that DAD can use my mistakes to carry out His plans. As I continue to go to the next level, my eyes are on being a kingdom builder for God. What I experienced was a benefit and God will add to it to accomplish His purpose. "And I am sure that God who began the good work within you will keep right on helping you grow in His grace until His task within you is finally finished on that day when Jesus Christ returns." Philippians 1:6 (TLB)

Be encouraged and do not skip the process. Walk it out, cry it out, think it out and then release it to your Higher Power.

## Peace

**"I am leaving you with a gift, peace of mind and heart! And the peace I give isn't fragile like the peace the world gives. So don't be troubled or afraid." John 14:27 (TLB)**

# ABOUT THE AUTHOR

Joanne McCrae is a quiet woman with a sturdy resolve. She has over 25 years of in-depth experience in highly responsible positions requiring significant *interpersonal and communication* skills. She is valued by many for her ability to organize her work and to successfully analyze issues for resolution. She caringly engages with individuals, which has sharpened her counseling skills in *listening, providing feedback,* and *creating positive outcomes* for those impacted by early traumatic experiences.

Due to the absence of her biological father, Joanne experienced challenges with abandonment and rejection that often left her feeling unwanted. Through each painful experience, she came into a greater awareness of who she was becoming. Rather than wallow in a web of sadness and disappointment, she developed a desire to understand the love of her Heavenly Father. Her experiences, while at times painful, were the catalyst that the Lord used for her to write this book with the sole purpose of encouraging the younger and older generations to understand who they are, learn to love themselves beyond the disappointments, and identify their God-given life purpose.

> **Life Scripture:**
> "And He said to them, 'Why did you seek Me?
> Did you not know that I must be about My Father's business?'"
> Luke 2:49 (NKJV)

www.ingramcontent.com/pod-product-compliance
Lightning Source LLC
Chambersburg PA
CBHW071759040426
42446CB00012B/2626